Merry & BRIGHT

A Keepsake Journal of
Family Christmas Memories

Castle Point Books
New York

The most beautiful things are not associated with money; **THEY ARE MEMORIES AND MOMENTS.** *If you don't celebrate those, they can pass you by.* —ALEK WEK

www.castlepointbooks.com

The Castle Point Books trademark is owned by Castle Point Publications, LLC.
Castle Point books are published and distributed by St. Martin's Press.

ISBN 978-1-250-22875-8

Design by Katie Jennings Campbell

Images used under license from Shutterstock.com

Our books may be purchased in bulk for promotional, educational, or business use. Please contact
your local bookseller or the Macmillan Corporate and Premium Sales Department at
1-800-221-7945, extension 5442, or by email at MacmillanSpecialMarkets@macmillan.com.

First Edition: October 2019

10 9 8 7 6 5 4 3 2 1

CAPTURE *the* MEMORIES & MOMENTS

Christmas is a special time to...

Wonder at the everyday miracles all around us.

Wrap our arms around the true gifts in our lives.

Celebrate and share love, peace, and warmth in our world.

But the season—and the feelings it brings—don't need to fade away when the decorations come down! Creating a Christmas keepsake journal is a simple but powerful way to hold onto all the magical memories and moments. Holidays past come alive with the help of your new *Merry & Bright* keepsake journal.

Throughout and right after the holiday season, just spend a few moments each day in these pages. Easy prompts help you capture 10 years of Christmas highlights in words, pictures, recipes, and more, so special moments live on for you and generations to come. It's a meaningful family tradition guaranteed to extend the heart of the holiday and bring focus to all the gifts in our lives.

OUR Christmas CELEBRATION

Year:

Events we attended during the season that especially filled us with holiday spirit:

_____

_____

_____

New movies we discovered or old movies we shared with someone new:

_____

_____

_____

Special books we read (or reread):

_____

_____

The song(s) that capture the heart of this year's holiday season:

_____

_____

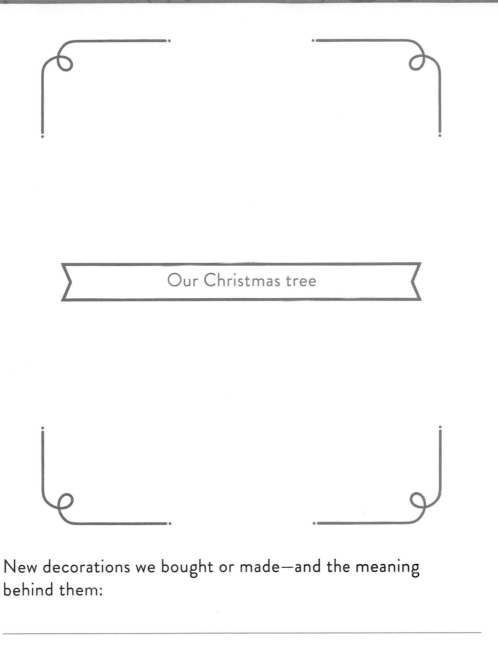

Our Christmas tree

New decorations we bought or made—and the meaning behind them:

_____

_____

The story of one special, longtime tradition we celebrated:

_____

_____

_____

_____

_____

The story of a new family tradition that was born:

_____

_____

_____

_____

_____

_____

_____

The Christmas greeting (card/letter) we sent out

The greeting we received that brought the biggest smile:

_____

_____

_____

_____

_____

GIFTS SHARED

GIFT	WHAT	TO	FROM
Favorite given			
Favorite received			
Most unexpected			
Funniest			
Best homemade			

Acts of kindness and charitable donations that shared the holiday spirit:

_____

_____

_____

_____

Special trips, parties, and visitors we enjoyed:

_____

_____

Making memories

A moment (big or little) I want to always remember:

_____

_____

THIS HOLIDAY IN HISTORY

Save
a stamp
here

New, popular, even crazy gifts and decorations:

_____

_____

Remembering the day's news headlines:

_____

_____

Our weather was:

_____

_____

My favorite moments of Christmas Eve:

_____

_____

The "gifts" of Christmas day that will remain with me always:

_____

_____

How we spent New Year's Eve, including what happened at midnight:

_____

_____

Holiday fun and togetherness

OUR HOME THIS HOLIDAY SEASON

SIGHTS	SCENTS	TOUCHES

What I'm most thankful for this Christmas season:

_____

_____

_____

_____

_____

_____

_____

Special foods we shared throughout the season:

_____

_____

_____

Our main holiday menu:

_____

_____

_____

A family-favorite holiday recipe:

Recipe _____

_____

_____

_____

_____

_____

_____

_____

How I will remember this year's holiday season:

_____

_____

_____

_____

_____

_____

The photo that captures it best!

My hopes for the new year for myself and our family:

_____

_____

_____

_____

_____

_____

_____

_____

_____

_____

OUR Christmas CELEBRATION

Year:

Events we attended during the season that especially filled us with holiday spirit:

_____

_____

_____

New movies we discovered or old movies we shared with someone new:

_____

_____

_____

Special books we read (or reread):

_____

_____

_____

The song(s) that capture the heart of this year's holiday season:

_____

_____

Our Christmas tree

New decorations we bought or made—and the meaning behind them:

_____

_____

The story of one special, longtime tradition we celebrated:

_____

_____

_____

_____

_____

_____

The story of a new family tradition that was born:

_____

_____

_____

_____

_____

_____

_____

The Christmas greeting (card/letter) we sent out

The greeting we received that brought the biggest smile:

_____

_____

_____

_____

_____

GIFTS SHARED

GIFT	WHAT	TO	FROM
Favorite given			
Favorite received			
Most unexpected			
Funniest			
Best homemade			

Acts of kindness and charitable donations that shared the holiday spirit:

_____

_____

_____

_____

_____

_____

_____

Special trips, parties, and visitors we enjoyed:

_____

_____

Making memories

A moment (big or little) I want to always remember:

_____

_____

THIS HOLIDAY IN HISTORY

Save
a stamp
here

New, popular, even crazy gifts and decorations:

_____

_____

Remembering the day's news headlines:

_____

_____

Our weather was:

_____

_____

My favorite moments of Christmas Eve:

_____

_____

The "gifts" of Christmas day that will remain with me always:

_____

_____

How we spent New Year's Eve, including what happened at midnight:

_____

_____

Holiday fun and togetherness

OUR HOME THIS HOLIDAY SEASON

SIGHTS	SCENTS	TOUCHES

What I'm most thankful for this Christmas season:

_____

_____

_____

_____

_____

_____

_____

Special foods we shared throughout the season:

_____

_____

_____

Our main holiday menu:

_____

_____

_____

A family-favorite holiday recipe:

Recipe _____

_____

_____

_____

_____

_____

_____

_____

How I will remember this year's holiday season:

_____

_____

_____

_____

_____

_____

_____

The photo that captures it best!

My hopes for the new year for myself and our family:

_____

_____

_____

_____

_____

_____

_____

_____

_____

_____

_____

OUR Christmas CELEBRATION

Year:

Events we attended during the season that especially filled us with holiday spirit:

_____

_____

_____

New movies we discovered or old movies we shared with someone new:

_____

_____

_____

Special books we read (or reread):

_____

_____

_____

The song(s) that capture the heart of this year's holiday season:

_____

_____

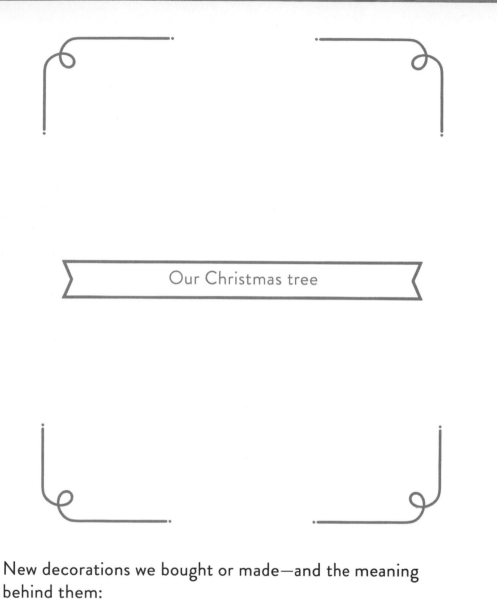

Our Christmas tree

New decorations we bought or made—and the meaning behind them:

_____

_____

The story of one special, longtime tradition we celebrated:

_____

_____

_____

_____

_____

_____

The story of a new family tradition that was born:

_____

_____

_____

_____

_____

_____

_____

_____

The Christmas greeting (card/letter) we sent out

The greeting we received that brought the biggest smile:

_____

_____

_____

_____

_____

GIFTS SHARED

GIFT	WHAT	TO	FROM
Favorite given			
Favorite received			
Most unexpected			
Funniest			
Best homemade			

Acts of kindness and charitable donations that shared the holiday spirit:

_____

_____

_____

_____

_____

_____

_____

Special trips, parties, and visitors we enjoyed:

_____

_____

Making memories

A moment (big or little) I want to always remember:

_____

_____

THIS HOLIDAY IN HISTORY

Save
a stamp
here

New, popular, even crazy gifts and decorations:

_____

_____

Remembering the day's news headlines:

_____

_____

Our weather was:

_____

_____

My favorite moments of Christmas Eve:

_____

_____

The "gifts" of Christmas day that will remain with me always:

_____

_____

How we spent New Year's Eve, including what happened at midnight:

_____

_____

Holiday fun and togetherness

OUR HOME THIS HOLIDAY SEASON

SIGHTS	SCENTS	TOUCHES

What I'm most thankful for this Christmas season:

Special foods we shared throughout the season:

_____

_____

_____

Our main holiday menu:

_____

_____

_____

A family-favorite holiday recipe:

Recipe _____

_____

_____

_____

_____

_____

_____

_____

How I will remember this year's holiday season:

_____

_____

_____

_____

_____

_____

The photo that captures it best!

My hopes for the new year for myself and our family:

_____

_____

_____

_____

_____

_____

_____

_____

_____

_____

_____

_____

_____

OUR Christmas CELEBRATION

Year:

Events we attended during the season that especially filled us with holiday spirit:

_____

_____

_____

New movies we discovered or old movies we shared with someone new:

_____

_____

_____

Special books we read (or reread):

_____

_____

_____

The song(s) that capture the heart of this year's holiday season:

_____

_____

Our Christmas tree

New decorations we bought or made—and the meaning behind them:

_____

_____

The story of one special, longtime tradition we celebrated:

_____

_____

_____

_____

_____

_____

The story of a new family tradition that was born:

_____

_____

_____

_____

_____

_____

_____

The Christmas greeting (card/letter) we sent out

The greeting we received that brought the biggest smile:

GIFTS SHARED

GIFT	WHAT	TO	FROM
Favorite given			
Favorite received			
Most unexpected			
Funniest			
Best homemade			

Acts of kindness and charitable donations that shared the holiday spirit:

_____

_____

_____

_____

Special trips, parties, and visitors we enjoyed:

_____

_____

Making memories

A moment (big or little) I want to always remember:

_____

_____

THIS HOLIDAY IN HISTORY

Save
a stamp
here

New, popular, even crazy gifts and decorations:

_____

_____

Remembering the day's news headlines:

_____

_____

Our weather was:

_____

_____

My favorite moments of Christmas Eve:

_____

_____

The "gifts" of Christmas day that will remain with me always:

_____

_____

How we spent New Year's Eve, including what happened at midnight:

_____

_____

Holiday fun and togetherness

OUR HOME THIS HOLIDAY SEASON

SIGHTS	SCENTS	TOUCHES

What I'm most thankful for this Christmas season:

_____

_____

_____

_____

_____

_____

Special foods we shared throughout the season:

_____

_____

_____

Our main holiday menu:

_____

_____

_____

A family-favorite holiday recipe:

Recipe _____

_____

_____

_____

_____

_____

_____

_____

How I will remember this year's holiday season:

_____

_____

_____

_____

_____

_____

_____

The photo that captures it best!

My hopes for the new year for myself and our family:

_____

_____

_____

_____

_____

_____

_____

_____

_____

_____

_____

_____

OUR
Christmas
CELEBRATION

Year:

Events we attended during the season that especially filled us with holiday spirit:

_____

_____

_____

New movies we discovered or old movies we shared with someone new:

_____

_____

_____

Special books we read (or reread):

_____

_____

_____

The song(s) that capture the heart of this year's holiday season:

_____

_____

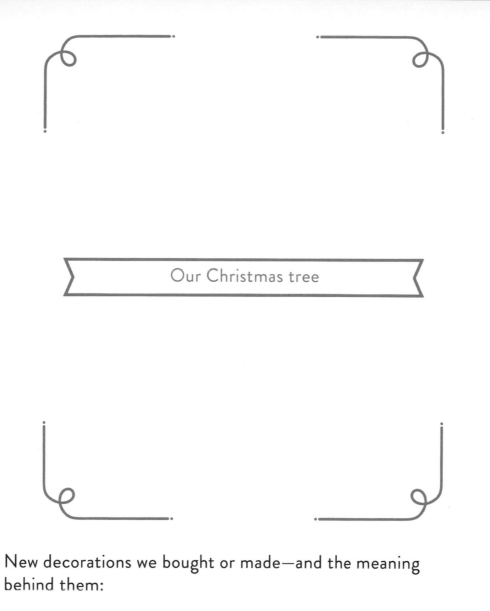

Our Christmas tree

New decorations we bought or made—and the meaning behind them:

_____

_____

The story of one special, longtime tradition we celebrated:

_____

_____

_____

_____

_____

_____

The story of a new family tradition that was born:

_____

_____

_____

_____

_____

_____

_____

_____

The Christmas greeting (card/letter) we sent out

The greeting we received that brought the biggest smile:

_____

_____

_____

_____

_____

GIFTS SHARED

GIFT	WHAT	TO	FROM
Favorite given			
Favorite received			
Most unexpected			
Funniest			
Best homemade			

Acts of kindness and charitable donations that shared the holiday spirit:

_____

_____

_____

_____

_____

_____

_____

Special trips, parties, and visitors we enjoyed:

_____

_____

Making memories

A moment (big or little) I want to always remember:

_____

_____

THIS HOLIDAY IN HISTORY

Save
a stamp
here

New, popular, even crazy gifts and decorations:

_____

_____

Remembering the day's news headlines:

_____

_____

Our weather was:

_____

_____

My favorite moments of Christmas Eve:

_____

_____

The "gifts" of Christmas day that will remain with me always:

_____

_____

How we spent New Year's Eve, including what happened at midnight:

_____

_____

Holiday fun and togetherness

 # OUR HOME THIS HOLIDAY SEASON

SIGHTS	SCENTS	TOUCHES

What I'm most thankful for this Christmas season:

_____

_____

_____

_____

_____

_____

_____

Special foods we shared throughout the season:

_____

_____

_____

Our main holiday menu:

_____

_____

_____

A family-favorite holiday recipe:

Recipe _____
_____
_____
_____
_____
_____
_____
_____
_____

How I will remember this year's holiday season:

_____

_____

_____

_____

_____

_____

The photo that captures it best!

My hopes for the new year for myself and our family:

_____

_____

_____

_____

_____

_____

_____

_____

_____

_____

_____

_____

OUR Christmas CELEBRATION

Year:

Events we attended during the season that especially filled us with holiday spirit:

_____

_____

_____

New movies we discovered or old movies we shared with someone new:

_____

_____

_____

Special books we read (or reread):

_____

_____

_____

The song(s) that capture the heart of this year's holiday season:

_____

_____

_____

Our Christmas tree

New decorations we bought or made—and the meaning behind them:

_____

_____

The story of one special, longtime tradition we celebrated:

_____

_____

_____

_____

_____

_____

The story of a new family tradition that was born:

_____

_____

_____

_____

_____

_____

_____

> The Christmas greeting (card/letter) we sent out

The greeting we received that brought the biggest smile:

_____

_____

_____

_____

_____

GIFTS SHARED

GIFT	WHAT	TO	FROM
Favorite given			
Favorite received			
Most unexpected			
Funniest			
Best homemade			

Acts of kindness and charitable donations that shared the holiday spirit:

_____

_____

_____

_____

_____

_____

_____

Special trips, parties, and visitors we enjoyed:

_____

_____

Making memories

A moment (big or little) I want to always remember:

_____

_____

THIS HOLIDAY IN HISTORY

Save
a stamp
here

New, popular, even crazy gifts and decorations:

_____

_____

Remembering the day's news headlines:

_____

_____

Our weather was:

_____

_____

My favorite moments of Christmas Eve:

_____

_____

The "gifts" of Christmas day that will remain with me always:

_____

_____

How we spent New Year's Eve, including what happened at midnight:

_____

_____

Holiday fun and togetherness

OUR HOME THIS HOLIDAY SEASON

SIGHTS	SCENTS	TOUCHES

What I'm most thankful for this Christmas season:

_____

_____

_____

_____

_____

_____

Special foods we shared throughout the season:

_____

_____

_____

Our main holiday menu:

_____

_____

_____

A family-favorite holiday recipe:

Recipe
_____
_____
_____
_____
_____
_____
_____
_____

How I will remember this year's holiday season:

_____

_____

_____

_____

_____

_____

The photo that captures it best!

My hopes for the new year for myself and our family:

_____

_____

_____

_____

_____

_____

_____

_____

_____

_____

_____

_____

_____

_____

OUR Christmas CELEBRATION

Year:

Events we attended during the season that especially filled us with holiday spirit:

_____

_____

_____

New movies we discovered or old movies we shared with someone new:

_____

_____

_____

Special books we read (or reread):

_____

_____

_____

The song(s) that capture the heart of this year's holiday season:

_____

_____

Our Christmas tree

New decorations we bought or made—and the meaning behind them:

_____

_____

The story of one special, longtime tradition we celebrated:

_____

_____

_____

_____

_____

_____

_____

The story of a new family tradition that was born:

_____

_____

_____

_____

_____

_____

_____

_____

The Christmas greeting (card/letter) we sent out

The greeting we received that brought the biggest smile:

_____

_____

_____

_____

_____

GIFTS SHARED

GIFT	WHAT	TO	FROM
Favorite given			
Favorite received			
Most unexpected			
Funniest			
Best homemade			

Acts of kindness and charitable donations that shared the holiday spirit:

_____

_____

_____

_____

_____

_____

_____

Special trips, parties, and visitors we enjoyed:

_____

_____

Making memories

A moment (big or little) I want to always remember:

_____

_____

THIS HOLIDAY IN HISTORY

Save
a stamp
here

New, popular, even crazy gifts and decorations:

_____

_____

Remembering the day's news headlines:

_____

_____

Our weather was:

_____

_____

My favorite moments of Christmas Eve:

_____

_____

The "gifts" of Christmas day that will remain with me always:

_____

_____

How we spent New Year's Eve, including what happened at midnight:

_____

_____

Holiday fun and togetherness

OUR HOME THIS HOLIDAY SEASON

SIGHTS	SCENTS	TOUCHES

What I'm most thankful for this Christmas season:

_____

_____

_____

_____

_____

_____

Special foods we shared throughout the season:

_____

_____

_____

Our main holiday menu:

_____

_____

_____

A family-favorite holiday recipe:

Recipe _____

_____

_____

_____

_____

_____

_____

_____

How I will remember this year's holiday season:

_____

_____

_____

_____

_____

_____

The photo that captures it best!

My hopes for the new year for myself and our family:

_____

_____

_____

_____

_____

_____

_____

_____

_____

_____

_____

_____

_____

OUR Christmas CELEBRATION

Year:

Events we attended during the season that especially filled us with holiday spirit:

_____

_____

_____

New movies we discovered or old movies we shared with someone new:

_____

_____

_____

Special books we read (or reread):

_____

_____

_____

The song(s) that capture the heart of this year's holiday season:

_____

_____

Our Christmas tree

New decorations we bought or made—and the meaning behind them:

_____

_____

The story of one special, longtime tradition we celebrated:

_____

_____

_____

_____

_____

_____

The story of a new family tradition that was born:

_____

_____

_____

_____

_____

_____

_____

The Christmas greeting (card/letter) we sent out

The greeting we received that brought the biggest smile:

GIFTS SHARED

GIFT	WHAT	TO	FROM
Favorite given			
Favorite received			
Most unexpected			
Funniest			
Best homemade			

Acts of kindness and charitable donations that shared the holiday spirit:

_____

_____

_____

_____

_____

_____

_____

Special trips, parties, and visitors we enjoyed:

_____

_____

Making memories

A moment (big or little) I want to always remember:

_____

_____

THIS HOLIDAY IN HISTORY

Save
a stamp
here

New, popular, even crazy gifts and decorations:

_____

_____

Remembering the day's news headlines:

_____

_____

Our weather was:

_____

_____

My favorite moments of Christmas Eve:

_____

_____

The "gifts" of Christmas day that will remain with me always:

_____

_____

How we spent New Year's Eve, including what happened at midnight:

_____

_____

Holiday fun and togetherness

OUR HOME THIS HOLIDAY SEASON

SIGHTS	SCENTS	TOUCHES

What I'm most thankful for this Christmas season:

_____

_____

_____

_____

_____

_____

Special foods we shared throughout the season:

_____

_____

_____

Our main holiday menu:

_____

_____

_____

A family-favorite holiday recipe:

Recipe _____

_____

_____

_____

_____

_____

_____

_____

How I will remember this year's holiday season:

_____

_____

_____

_____

_____

_____

The photo that captures it best!

My hopes for the new year for myself and our family:

_____

_____

_____

_____

_____

_____

_____

_____

_____

_____

_____

_____

OUR Christmas CELEBRATION

Year:

Events we attended during the season that especially filled us with holiday spirit:

_____

_____

_____

New movies we discovered or old movies we shared with someone new:

_____

_____

_____

Special books we read (or reread):

_____

_____

The song(s) that capture the heart of this year's holiday season:

_____

_____

_____

Our Christmas tree

New decorations we bought or made—and the meaning behind them:

_____

_____

The story of one special, longtime tradition we celebrated:

_____

_____

_____

_____

_____

_____

The story of a new family tradition that was born:

_____

_____

_____

_____

_____

_____

_____

The Christmas greeting (card/letter) we sent out

The greeting we received that brought the biggest smile:

_____

_____

_____

_____

_____

GIFTS SHARED

GIFT	WHAT	TO	FROM
Favorite given			
Favorite received			
Most unexpected			
Funniest			
Best homemade			

Acts of kindness and charitable donations that shared the holiday spirit:

_____

_____

_____

_____

_____

_____

_____

Special trips, parties, and visitors we enjoyed:

_____

_____

Making memories

A moment (big or little) I want to always remember:

_____

_____

THIS HOLIDAY IN HISTORY

Save a stamp here

New, popular, even crazy gifts and decorations:

_____

_____

Remembering the day's news headlines:

_____

_____

Our weather was:

_____

_____

My favorite moments of Christmas Eve:

_____

_____

The "gifts" of Christmas day that will remain with me always:

_____

_____

How we spent New Year's Eve, including what happened at midnight:

_____

_____

Holiday fun and togetherness

OUR HOME THIS HOLIDAY SEASON

SIGHTS	SCENTS	TOUCHES

What I'm most thankful for this Christmas season:

_____

_____

_____

_____

_____

_____

Special foods we shared throughout the season:

_____

_____

_____

Our main holiday menu:

_____

_____

_____

A family-favorite holiday recipe:

Recipe _____

_____

_____

_____

_____

_____

_____

_____

_____

How I will remember this year's holiday season:

_____

_____

_____

_____

_____

_____

The photo that captures it best!

My hopes for the new year for myself and our family:

_____

_____

_____

_____

_____

_____

_____

_____

_____

_____

_____

_____

OUR Christmas CELEBRATION

Year:

Events we attended during the season that especially filled us with holiday spirit:

_____

_____

_____

New movies we discovered or old movies we shared with someone new:

_____

_____

_____

Special books we read (or reread):

_____

_____

_____

The song(s) that capture the heart of this year's holiday season:

_____

_____

_____

Our Christmas tree

New decorations we bought or made—and the meaning behind them:

_____

_____

The story of one special, longtime tradition we celebrated:

_____

_____

_____

_____

_____

_____

The story of a new family tradition that was born:

_____

_____

_____

_____

_____

_____

_____

The Christmas greeting (card/letter) we sent out

The greeting we received that brought the biggest smile:

_____

_____

_____

_____

_____

GIFTS SHARED

GIFT	WHAT	TO	FROM
Favorite given			
Favorite received			
Most unexpected			
Funniest			
Best homemade			

Acts of kindness and charitable donations that shared the holiday spirit:

_____

_____

_____

_____

Special trips, parties, and visitors we enjoyed:

_____

_____

Making memories

A moment (big or little) I want to always remember:

_____

_____

THIS HOLIDAY IN HISTORY

| Save a stamp here |

New, popular, even crazy gifts and decorations:

_____

_____

Remembering the day's news headlines:

_____

_____

Our weather was:

_____

_____

My favorite moments of Christmas Eve:

_____

_____

The "gifts" of Christmas day that will remain with me always:

_____

_____

How we spent New Year's Eve, including what happened at midnight:

_____

_____

Holiday fun and togetherness

OUR HOME THIS HOLIDAY SEASON

SIGHTS	SCENTS	TOUCHES

What I'm most thankful for this Christmas season:

_____

_____

_____

_____

_____

_____

_____

Special foods we shared throughout the season:

_____

_____

_____

Our main holiday menu:

_____

_____

_____

A family-favorite holiday recipe:

Recipe _____

_____

_____

_____

_____

_____

_____

How I will remember this year's holiday season:

_____

_____

_____

_____

_____

_____

The photo that captures it best!

My hopes for the new year for myself and our family:

_____

_____

_____

_____

_____

_____

_____

_____

_____

_____

_____